The Life That's Chosen Me

From Russia with Love?

Rachelle Rasolofo-Czerwinski

The Life That's Chosen Me

Tellwell Talent
www.tellwell.ca

ISBN
978-0-2288-4602-4 (Paperback)

The Life That's Chosen Me

A Family Memoir

From Russia with Love?

2003-2005

TABLE OF CONTENTS

FOREWORD

The chapter you are about to read is the final leg of our family's journey across six countries and three continents, in the service of the United Nations' World Food Programme (WFP) before finally returning to take up a permanent home in Canada. Our family of four consisted of my husband Chris, Country Representative of WFP, Russia, myself as a trailing spouse, my son Michael, our rebellious teen at that time and his younger brother Nicholas, non-verbal and with significant special needs. When I began to share our journey, I chose to write about our time in Russia first because in remembering, this chapter of our nomadic life was the most difficult on a background of a brutal war and overt racism. During our two years there I felt exhausted, frustrated, lonely, uprooted, vulnerable and even scared.

I wrote this chapter first as it was the freshest in my memory and perhaps also to unpack the pain and finally settle down.

> "When the memory looks for dead wood,
> it brings back the bundle it fancies."
>
> African proverb

Vancouver, August 2022

WHAT AM I DOING HERE?

It was mid-August 2003 and I am staring out the window into the greyness of our new life, watching the rain relentlessly spattering on it with no end in sight. We had just moved from Cairo to Moscow on our seventh posting abroad. I felt sad about leaving Egypt. During my five years there, I made many good friends, both Egyptians and foreigners, and had done so many things I was proud of. I contributed to the first ever Directory for Special Needs in the country, taught bilingual jewelry-making classes and chaired the United Nations Spouses Association.

Egypt had become my home and leaving for Moscow was very difficult.

We had hoped that by arriving in Moscow in mid-August we would get a taste of the Russian summer. As luck would have it, that summer of 2003 was one of the worst in Russian history.. We were staying in this apartment/hotel in a gloomy Moscow suburb and it rained every day for two weeks. Some days, the wind was so strong I had difficulty walking with Nicholas with his unsteady gait. So, we just walked in the hallway and I would wait for Chris to come home so we could do some errands. About three days after we arrived, Chris announced excitedly that he had to leave for a two-week mission in the North Caucasus!

I gasped, "You're leaving us so soon? For two weeks? But we just arrived!"

"It's my job, Rachelle, part of why we are here."

Yes, that was true, the reason we were in Russia was for Chris' job and his job was to deliver food aid to war-torn Chechnya.

My job, on the other hand, was to cater to the needs of the family and maybe, as the last priority, to my own needs.

So, there I was, in a new country with a severely disabled child and a teenager! We did not speak the language; we did not have a home or a car or any friends. I felt miserable and lonely.

For the first time in our nomadic life, I did not feel the familiar excitement about moving to a new country. I felt tired just thinking about making new friends, looking for a new school for Michael and especially finding support and services for Nicholas. I had always known that eventually we would leave Egypt but now that we were here, I found myself wishing we had stayed in Egypt or gone to Indonesia. But, unlike me, towards the end of our stay, Chris had developed an intense dislike for Egypt because of the incessant infighting amongst his staff. He was also frustrated by the slow progress on his projects, the politics of international development aid, and above all, he hated our last landlord, a former Egyptian army colonel who had trained in Russia. Chris had found our first dwelling in Cairo on a very busy one way street and we were getting along very well with Mahmoud, our landlord. But after four years, I wanted to move into a quieter neighbourhood, more residential, closer to our kids' school. To accomplish this, I took entire care of the move. Yet, Chris still resented it, so when anything went wrong in the house, it was the landlord's fault and my fault. One example of this was when we had issues with the electrical system at the house. Chris pestered the landlord daily to come and fix it. The landlord dragged his feet for the longest time and I was wedged in between trying my best to keep the peace.

Chris had filed his preference list for our next posting: Country Director in Russia or Deputy Country Director in Indonesia. He wanted Russia, where he would be the boss, while I preferred Indonesia for its similar climate and hospitable culture to Madagascar, my home country.

When Chris announced that our next post would be Russia, I shook my head:

"Russia? Nyet, it's too cold!"

Chris did his best to convince me, saying it wouldn't be that bad and that living in an European country, we would be close to places like Berlin and Paris. Finally, I gave in knowing how much it meant for Chris to be the boss.

All of this reminded me that, of course, Chris' career was the most important thing, and I was just a *trailing spouse*, a type of modern day, privileged immigrant. Yes, I knew the challenges ahead of me. I will be arriving in a new country. I will have to learn a new language, find a school for Nicholas with his multiple needs, and make new friends. On the other hand, I arrived with a diplomatic visa and I had the support of Chris' office. I suppose I really should have felt more cheerful.

We left Cairo and, after spending a short summer in Vancouver with my parents-in-law, we arrived in Moscow in mid-August. Michael's school, the Anglo-American School of Moscow, started soon after we arrived.

After Chris left, I sat at the kitchen table feeding Nicholas, feeling empty and alone, and staring at the pouring rain outside wondering "*What am I doing here?*"

I had been a trailing spouse for close to 20 years, and for the first time I felt defeated, lonely and tired. Tired of starting over again in another country, looking for schools, learning yet another language and finding friends. I had never felt this way before, but I felt it deeply in Moscow.

Moscow was a completely different experience for me and I wondered why. There was the weather of course, which was dramatically different from Egypt. In Egypt it rained 5 days a year and the rest of the time was dry, warm and sunny. I also realized that our two previous postings, Cairo and before that Beijing, had one significant advantage: Help was available upon arrival.

When we moved to Beijing from Rome, Italy, I took Barbara, Nicholas' Italian support worker with us for our first three months; in addition, we hired Mrs. Guo from our predecessor as our house helper. Four years later, when we moved from China to Egypt, I convinced Mrs. Guo to come and stay with us for the first three months. In Moscow, however, I had nobody to help with Nicholas or with the move. How had I let this happen? Nicholas was 15 years old and needed support to do everything from getting dressed to eating. He could not shower on his own and he needed help in the bathroom. He also could not walk without support and was non-verbal. As his mom, I understood his way of communicating but he was not easily understood by those who did not know him.

Eventually, things did settle down even with Chris away. Michael rode a bus to and from the Anglo-American school every day which gave me time to keep searching for an appropriate school for Nicholas. I did not know whether we would ever find one. He could not go to a Russian public school with other students because there was no inclusive education. No one at Chris' office knew of a private school for special needs students. Chris' executive assistant, a lovely middle-aged Russian woman named Tatiana Chubrikova, had been calling around for me but had found nothing. While we waited to hear from her, every morning after breakfast Nicholas and I would go for a long walk in the neighbourhood and come back around lunchtime.

Our apartment-hotel was not located in a residential area but rather in a blue-collar suburban part of town. We were surrounded by tall grey buildings, next to a large, busy, treeless road. There were no nearby parks or stores for us to explore.

We walked bravely into the wind, the rain and above all, the stares of the people we encountered. Here we were in the streets of Moscow, a boy in a wheelchair and his mother, a woman of colour. People, old and young, men and women, whether on the sidewalk, in buses or cars, would stare at us. I did not know whether I should have felt scared or annoyed at all the attention, but I was starting to feel seriously depressed.

Shortly after developing our walking routine, I attended a meeting that was part of our orientation package, organized by an expatriate women's group to help newcomers. The meeting was held in a posh downtown hotel where Igor, a young, neatly dressed, soft-spoken Russian man taught us about the dos and don'ts of Russian life.

I only remember the don'ts:

- Do not greet people on the threshold of your door, it brings bad luck. Greet them either outside your door or once they come inside.
- Do not bring chrysanthemums as hostess gifts because they are the flowers of choice for funerals.

"There are a few important dates to remember as well," Igor continued, "March 8th, International Women's Day, is one of them. Every man offers red roses to all the women in his life: his mother, his wife, his mistress, his sisters, his female teachers etc and if you don't, you are in real trouble! And on or around the 20th of April," he added, if you are of Asian or African descent, try not to go out in the streets. If you do, try to avoid any groups of young men clad in black jackets with high boots".

There were a few African and Asian women in our group. We looked at each other hesitantly, then one of us raised her hand and asked: "And why is that?"

The presenter sighed, slightly embarrassed.

"The 20th of April is Hitler's birthday and there are skinheads and neo-Nazis who want to celebrate and mark the day, carrying chains and wearing brass knuckles."

When he saw our puzzled looks, he hesitated: "Well, it is just better to avoid them..." He could not look at us and just kept staring down at his shiny black shoes.

I shivered. Again, what was I doing here as a dark-skinned mother of a disabled young man?

I wanted to know more about racist attacks, so I started reading the Moscow Times-the local English language newspaper, more closely. I was shocked to read that incidents of racial hatred and anti-Semitism happened every day. African students would get beaten up on the underground train late at night, a young girl from the Caucasus was stabbed at the market as she was walking with her parents and one of my husband's colleagues from Nepal had to run for his life.

What am I doing here? I kept asking myself. I felt terrified and vulnerable.

Moscow was not right for me or for our sons. I did not feel safe here nor welcome or accepted.

On the way home from the orientation meeting, I couldn't think of anything else except Indonesia and how I felt slighted by having to move to this backwards, dangerous country. Having to stay in your house on April 20th because of Hitler's birthday, was unbelievable! Russia was Chris' choice not mine. My choice was Indonesia. I did not care that Chris would have been second in charge in Indonesia. Indonesia would have been warm with hibiscus flowers and green lawns. I would have fit in so much easier with the locals who look more like me. In fact, our ancestors in Madagascar came from Indonesia! Moreover, in Indonesia, I would have had help as I did in China and Egypt. I came home feeling very sorry for myself and overcome by all the challenges – I just wanted to go home but where was home for us? Where was home for me?

I was born in Madagascar, as far away as you can get from Canada! My father was an officer in the French Army before the country became independent in 1960. Then when Madagascar became independent, the newly formed government asked Malagasy officers in the French army whether they wanted to come back to Madagascar and form the National Army. My father joined the first group of officers. I had done my primary classes in Southern France with my siblings and when we returned to Madagascar I had to learn Malagasy.

Later on, after graduating from high school, I went to the University of Madagascar, the only university in the country, located in Antananarivo, the capital city. I studied economics and political science, went to Kenya for a year to practice my English, came back, got a job with Air France, the French airline, and one day, Chris walked into the agency to book a ticket for Cameroon, West Africa. He came every day for the next two weeks, always with some little change in the departure date or the return date. But whenever he walked in, my colleagues would smile and wink at each other: "Here comes Rachelle's Canadian"!!!

Two years later, in June 1984, I arrived in Vancouver, to get married and start a new life in Canada. Six months later, Chris got a job with the World Food Programme, a

United Nations agency that specialized in Food Aid. So we left Canada to join our first job posting in Segou, a small town in Mali, West Africa. We stayed two years in Mali followed by two years in Djibouti, East Africa, had our two kids while we were in Djibouti although they were born in Vancouver at Grace Hospital on Oak Street.

Nicholas developed his seizure disorder shortly after he got his first childhood vaccine. He got his first set of vaccines when he was two months old, one month earlier than he should normally have. But we were eager to join Chris after three months in Vancouver, one month before the birth and two months after. His neurologist at Children Hospital in Vancouver later explained that the vaccines were not the cause but more likely the catalyst for the seizures to happen. He was diagnosed with a rare condition called West Syndrome and infantile spasms affecting about one child per 100,000 births. It could not really be treated in Djibouti so Chris' organization decided to transfer us to their headquarters in Rome, Italy.

Italy was followed by four years in China, five years in Egypt and two years in Russia.

Now, back to Russia! Back to reality!

One morning Nicholas and I went for our usual walk. We would regularly sit on a bench under a covered bus shelter to watch the buses go by. This was great entertainment for Nicholas, but it was not such great entertainment for me, as I tried to ignore all the stares from the bus passengers looking down on us from their windows

It did, however, give me a glimpse of daily life in Russia.

That morning, another miserable gloomy morning, at about 10 am, a man who reeked of vodka came to our bus shelter looking for empty liquor bottles. My research on Russia told me about the huge problem of alcoholism here. Alcohol consumption in Russia is among the highest in the world, with an annual per capita consumption of 20.1 litres, the fourth highest volume in Europe. In comparison, Canada and the United States consume about 13.7 litres of pure alcohol per person per year. One in five men dies from alcohol-related causes. In Russia, children as young as 11 are addicted and considered alcoholics. Booze is sold freely at each street corner; nobody asks for identification and apparently Mikhail Gorbachev lost the Russian people's approval when he started to talk about regulating the sale of vodka. Many drink alcohol to forget the harsh reality of their lives or to keep warm or both. And every year when spring comes and snow melts, there are always bodies that appear in some of Moscow's ditches.

As we sat on our bench, everyone passing by stared at us. A bus stopped and a grey- haired lady, perhaps in her sixties, smiled warmly at us as she stepped from the bus onto the sidewalk. It felt strange as she was the first person who smiled at us in the two weeks we had been in Russia! Even more surprisingly, the woman came toward us, said something in Russian and blessed us. Yes, blessed us! She made the sign of the cross twice, once over my head and once over Nicholas' head. This lady was talking at the same time; maybe she was saying a prayer.

As I recovered from the shock, she looked into her bag, took out two sweets and gave one to each of us. (I still have these sweets preciously wrapped somewhere in a box)

She started to leave when suddenly as if she forgot something, she turned and came back to us, looked in her bag again and brought out a small bottle of water. I got worried. "Oh my gosh! She wants us to drink that water!"

Quickly, I was thinking of some polite way to not drink the water. But that water was not for drinking! She opened the bottle and she poured it over our heads and blessed us again! Before I could even respond, she was gone.

For a long time, Nicholas and I would take that same walk and sit on that bench looking for her to step out of that bus once more, but we never saw her again.

But I will always remember that woman as our Russian angel who gave us the most precious gift during some of my life's darkest moments: a smile and a blessing.

With Tatiana Chubrikova

A CHANGING FAMILY IN A CHANGING COUNTRY

It was the spring of 2004, our second year in Russia and over the weeks and months that followed, I swallowed my depression and got on with the business of life.. After being shown a dozen places, we had finally found an apartment for the family that was not in an expatriate ghetto and cost less than $15,000 a month!

Good Tatiana Chubrikova, Chris's executive assistant, also found a good school for Nicholas called St. George's School for Handicapped Children.

St. George's School followed Anthroposophy, started by Rudolf Steiner in the early 20th century. For example, the school only served vegetarian meals and advocated the use of natural materials: cotton, linen and wool were the materials of choice throughout the school. I later learned that Rudolf Steiner also believed in the superiority of the Aryan race but looking back I never saw anything coming from the school that could be interpreted as racial discrimination. Whenever we went there, we always felt welcome.

The schoolmaster had referred two women from the school to assist Nicholas: Anya and Masha. Anya was young and sweet, and she loved Nicholas like a younger brother. She was also tiny, under 5 feet tall and I was always amazed that Nicholas did not fall over her as they went downstairs every morning on their way to school.

Masha was older than Anya, Jewish and a single mother of an 8-year-old daughter. She was born in Moldova, formerly known as the Moldavian Soviet Socialist Republic when it was still part of Russia. She stayed a few months in Israel but returned, saying that Russia was her country. Masha knew all kinds of natural remedies for every ailment like applying slices of raw onion on your back to fight fever. She also taught me how to make Borscht, the red beet soup that Russians love. She usually wore Birkenstock shoes and used Aveda products so gradually she came to be known in our house as Ms. Birkenstock.

Our family was living on the second floor of an old building on Ostoshenka Street, not far from the famous Gorki Park. There was an elevator that did not come to our floor (it went up from the second floor) We were paying U.S $6,000 a month for this spacious three-bedroom apartment and Olga, our realtor thought it was a tremendous deal, as other expats were paying up to $15,000 monthly! Moscow was becoming as expensive as London or Tokyo! I knew our realtor had worked hard to find us a good place.

I remember the day I met Olga for the first time. The real estate agency had called earlier to say that they had a few places lined up for us to see and that they would be sending an agent to the hotel to pick me up at 3 pm.

At 3 pm, the agent called to say that she was waiting for me in the lobby, so I headed down and went straight to a blond woman who was obviously waiting for someone.

"Hi," I said with a smile, "You must be waiting for me!"

She appeared confused: "No, I am not waiting for you…"

I apologized and looked around in the lobby for someone appearing to wait for somebody but I did not see anyone so I went back to her with a smile:

"I think you ARE waiting for me…"

"No, she shook her head, I am not waiting for you. I am waiting for a Mrs. Czerwinski."

"Oh," I said triumphantly, "that's me, I am Rachelle Czerwinski!"

She almost choked from embarrassment and apologized profusely.

"I am so sorry, I did not know, please forgive me..."

It was awkward but I felt sorry for her. After all, it was partially my fault; I should have introduced myself first. Who would ever have guessed that someone named Rachelle Czerwinski would be a person of color? She probably expected a blond, blue-eyed and big-breasted Polish woman…

That day we looked at five apartments. There was a really nice one with three bedrooms and two bathrooms on Tverskaya Street, bright and roomy. Olga said Tverskaya is the most expensive shopping street in Moscow, the equivalent of the Champs-Elysees in Paris. So at $7,000 monthly it was a steal. As we drove around, she told me about her Nigerian boyfriend and how handsome he was with his dark skin.

When she dropped me off, I asked Said, our family driver, what he thought about the flat on Tverskaya Street. He said it is a very nice street but at night it can be noisy.

"How come, Saïd?"

"Well, Saïd replied with a smile, at night, it is one of the favorite streets for prostitutes because customers are wealthy in that area..."

"Hmm, I see…"

Well, I guess it really helps to have a local driver who knows the city!

When I told her this story, Masha, one of Nicholas' assistants, had a good laugh. For her, paying $7,000 a month for housing was in any case unthinkable. But it is also true that it was a steal in the expatriate rental market. Our friends who worked for private companies like Esso or Ford paid over $15,000 a month for their apartment and it was only slightly bigger than ours.

As Nicholas' life was becoming organized, I finally had the time and energy to take Russian lessons. This was a new language with a different alphabet. For example, the word "restaurant" was spelled *Pectopah,* and was pronounced "restaurant" (the Cyrillic letters were pronounced differently than English ones) so one word helped me remember eight letters of the Russian alphabet! I felt quite proud of myself.

I did not learn Russian as fast as Chinese or Arabic. I pondered whether my brain was getting rusty after 20 years living this nomadic life. I learned Chinese in China, Arabic in Egypt and Italian in Italy but Russian didn't happen as easily or quickly. So many things got in the way! A different way of living, the terrible weather, and the overt racism all left me feeling unsafe and made it much harder to learn. While learning Russian, I was pleasantly surprised to discover that many French words found their way into their vocabulary, thanks to Napoleon and his troops: chocolat, porte-monnaie (wallet), cauchemar (nightmare)...

On May 9, 2004, the Chechen president, Akhmad Kadyrov, had been assassinated by a landmine placed under a VIP stage during a World War II commemoration parade in Grozny, the capital of Chechnya. Chris' humanitarian work was to deliver food to Chechnya, but it was too dangerous to go there directly because of the war, so he was working from neighboring Ingushetia. Consequently, whatever happened in Chechnya impacted his work in Russia.

On September 1st of the same year, Chechen terrorists took 1,128 hostages, half of whom were children, in what was later known as the Beslan School hostage crisis. The hostage takers demanded the release of Chechen rebels imprisoned in Ingushetia and the independence of Chechnya from Russia. The siege lasted 3 days. On the third day of the standoff, Russian security forces stormed the building with the use of tanks, incendiary rockets and other heavy weapons. At least 385 hostages were killed including 186 children.

Despite the terrible events, we tried to live life as normally as possible: school, work, home.

Following the Beslan hostage crisis, Nestlé-Russia donated nine tons of high energy food to help feed the hostages: chocolate bars, cereal bars etc. Chris organized the air shipment to Vladikavkaz, the capital city of the Republic of North Ossetia, the closest airport to Beslan.

Later on his headquarters were appalled that he had dealings with Nestlé and that it will hurt their PR image.

Anyway it was too late, the food was distributed and Chris decided that sometimes the needs have to come before PR politics.

On the home side, Michael had started grade 11 at the Anglo-American School of Moscow. This would be his sixth school in 5 countries. He attended Il Cigno in Rome, Italy for kindergarten followed by Brittania International School for Grade 1. I remember when we left Italy for China in 1994, Mike was on a waitlist for Beijing International School. It was uncertain whether he would be accepted.

Fortunately, a new school, the Western Academy of Beijing, was being built. Soon after we arrived, Mike was able to start grade 2. Pat, the principal of Brittania, Mike's school in Italy, was amazed that our family would even consider leaving for China without first securing a spot in a school.

"You are so brave," she told me a week before departure day. "You can just leave the comfort of a home and old friends to engage in a new adventure, just like that, and so far away!"

Pat had come from England ten years ago and had married an Italian man like many British women do when they visit Italy. She used to say that Italy was exotic enough for her without the need to explore some faraway land.

After China, Mike was accepted at the Cairo American College for middle school. Halfway through middle school, however, he asked to complete his studies in Canada.

"I'm sick and tired of all this moving around, he said in a typical teenage manner. "I keep losing my friends and having to make new ones."

We could not really argue with that reasoning. After all, I often felt the same way! So, in the fall of 2001, Mike attended Grade 9 at Brentwood College on Vancouver Island while we remained in Cairo. He stayed there for Grade 9; his school reports had mixed reviews. He thrived academically and was even elected class valedictorian at the end of the year.

However, his behavior was another matter; maybe he just missed his family, but we do know that he spent a lot of time cleaning school bathrooms as punishment for his transgressions.

In the fall of 2002, he returned to Cairo American College for Grade 10.

Now he was looking forward to graduating from high school in Moscow. His year away in Canada had made him more appreciative of the comforts provided by expat life. In addition, he was pleased that the new principal of the Anglo-American School in Moscow was Drew Alexander, his former vice-principal from Cairo American College. Drew was very happy to reconnect with us at the Parent's meeting. "What a change from Cairo," he smiled. "There, no alcohol was allowed at meetings and here it is mandatory, not officially, but we know no Russian parent will come to a 'dry' gathering!"

The school was situated in a Moscow suburb, 45 minutes away from where we lived. At first, Alexei, one of the office drivers, drove Michael every morning and Mike would then return by public transit in the afternoon. But

I was so worried about racially motivated attacks that I asked Alexei to follow Mike on the underground train! It quickly appeared that this was not sustainable with respect to Alexei's time as well as Mike's pride. With some networking within the school, we arranged for Michael to share a taxi with Maria, the daughter of the Finnish military attaché who was living around the corner from our apartment.

During the spring break, the school organized a trip to the Ural Mountains for the grade 11 students and Mike had fallen head over heels for Sara*, a schoolmate from Bulgaria. (*Not her real name for privacy)

I was eager to know more "What does her dad do? And her mom?" I asked, "Where does she live? Is she a good student?"

Sara's dad was Purchasing Manager at Ikea. No, Mike could not tell me much about Sara's mom. He was mostly interested in Sara.

One Saturday afternoon, Mike went out with Sara somewhere in the city. Chris was away in Ingushetia but was to return that evening.

Around 7 pm, Mike called.

He asked, "Mom, is it ok to bring Sara home with me?"

I was perplexed "What do you mean Mike, can't she go home?"

"She can, but ...but it is easier for her to come home with me, her house is on the other side of the city and it is getting late. Don't worry, she already asked her mom and it's ok."

I hesitated. Mike had brought friends home overnight in the past, but *never* a girl.

Thoughts swirled in my head as I held the phone to my ear: *He is not 17 yet. He is too young to bring a girl home to spend the night! But if I say no, what would they do? Where would they go?* My fears grew with my thoughts about those racial attacks happening after dark.

I sighed, "I suppose you should better bring her here than be wandering God knows where. I will leave the key underneath the doormat."

Mike was jubilant: "Thank you, Mom. You're the best mom in the world!"

I did not really feel like meeting Sara. I still did not agree with her coming over and spending the night but what choice did I have?

This is so awkward, I thought, staring through the window into the cloudy skies. *What would other parents do?*

After tucking Nicholas in bed, I decided to go to bed early with the book I had started a few days before, Harper Lee's *To Kill a Mockingbird*. Around 9 pm, I heard the key in the door, I quickly turned off my light, pretending to be asleep. The front door opened and closed, some lights were turned on, someone flushed the toilet, and then silence and darkness fell over the house.

I had a hard time relaxing even with such a good book as Harper Lee's, wondering whether I had done the right thing, playing with different options, maybe I should have called Sara's parents, maybe I should have asked Chris for his advice, oh, so hard to be a good parent when you are faced with challenging situations. This was a new and challenging situation for any parent not to mention a parent in a foreign country, I needed to relax. I turned off my light, closed my eyes and tried to concentrate on listening to my breathing. I had gradually started to fall asleep, using the yoga breathing system: breathe in through your nose for four counts, hold for seven, and breathe out through your mouth for eight, 4-7-8, 4-7-8.... when I was interrupted by someone tiptoeing toward my bed.

"Mom," Mike whispered in my ear as he knelt down.

"Yes… Mike?"

"Mom? Where are the condoms?"

I froze. Pulling the bedsheets over my face, I wanted to scream "Noooo, this can't be happening... this cannot be happening to ME! This can't be happening to my baby!"

I gestured towards the other side of the bed in slow motion.

"Huh, in your dad's drawer," I whispered from under the sheet almost inaudibly.

"Thanks, Mom!" he exclaimed and, just like that, he was gone.

I remained motionless in bed, wondering if this had just been a bad dream. Could my baby be having sex just now, next to my bedroom, with someone who was a complete stranger to me?

I turned and tossed around, trying to sleep. Breathe in, hold, and breathe out, 4-7-8, 4-7-8...

It was close to midnight when Chris arrived from Ingushetia. He lay down next to me and turned on his bedside light.

"Everything all right here? I had a busy trip, I tell you," he sighed in a tired voice.

"Just don't go into Mike's bedroom," I whispered.

"I was not going to but why? Something happened? Is he sick?" Chris was suddenly concerned.

"No, he is not, I wish he were," I sounded irritated. "Just that there is a girl in there, with him, Sara is her name, that's all..."

"WHAT? How did this happen?" he exclaimed in a stage whisper.

"I'll explain tomorrow," I sighed. "I'm tired, I need to sleep - and by the way, he took your condoms. Why are you never around when I need you?"

The next morning when Chris got up to make coffee, Mike and Sara were already in the kitchen. Mike was making an omelette and Sara was chopping onions, tomatoes and green peppers. They seemed comfortable with each other, moving around one another with the kind of ease that usually comes when two people have spent the night together. Sara wore heavy make-up, she had multiple earrings and a ring in her nose.

"Good morning," I said with a forced smile.

"Morning Mom," Mike said cheerfully, planting a kiss on my cheek. "This is Sara," and he smiled his big charming smile.

I observed him from the corner of my eye, wondering to myself, *"Did he ever have sex before? Was last night his first time? Is this the same person as the child who used to giggle wildly when I threw him in the air?"* Suddenly he felt like a stranger to me.

"Let's put Vivaldi on," Chris said, his coffee mug in hand, "just like Opa would do on Sunday mornings, and we can roast a chicken tonight, just as Oma would do back home."

Chris entertained us with his latest story. He was in North Ossetia coming back from Chechnya. He and a Czech colleague from FAO, the Food and Agriculture Organization of the UN, were boarding an Antonov, an old model which had a ramp that you could close from the inside. It was the only door of the aircraft.

The crew had closed the door and passengers were just waiting to take off.

At that moment, they heard loud banging on the door with a slew of angry outbursts. It was the pilot who was outside having a smoke!

The Czech guy understood Russian and told Chris the language was pretty colorful!

Mike and Sara laughed wholeheartedly, I smiled and shook my head, still thinking of last night's event, as if wanting to forget a bad dream. The scene seemed like a normal Sunday family breakfast. Chris wanted to make it look like a normal Sunday morning, yet I knew that things would never be the same.

With Saïd, Public Works Engineer turned family driver, lucky for us

Nicholas and Masha

Cuddly moment with Anya

THE MOSCOW SOCIAL CLUB

In the name of "International Socialism," Russia offered modest scholarships to students from all over the world, so people from Asia, Africa and the Americas came to live and study. Most of them attended Patrice Lumumba University also called the Peoples' Friendship University in Moscow. Patrice Lumumba University was established in 1960 and became an integral part of the Soviet cultural policy in non-aligned countries from Asia, Africa and Latin America during the cold war and after. There were also international students at universities in other cities in Russia.

Their situation was ambiguous. On one hand, the government invited them by awarding them scholarships and on the other hand, part of the population (especially right-wing groups) shunned them. The Neo-Nazi Party was an official political organization here and they openly rejected foreigners, especially dark-skinned ones. Interestingly, they discriminated against Jews as well even though the Russian Jews looked very Russian to me. Many African students had Russian girlfriends, which the local society frowned upon, even more so when those couples had children. These mixed-race children were often bullied in schools and discriminated against and many ended in orphanages when their Russian mothers gave up their parental responsibilities under pressure from their families and a hostile society.

Our family was very fortunate to meet some of these former students because they helped us integrate into Russian culture.

One of them was Lalao, a student from Madagascar whose mother worked for the Malagasy Embassy. She became our first babysitter, and she was the one who introduced us to Saïd, our family driver in Russia. He was originally from Mahajanga, the biggest city on the west coast of Madagascar. He moved to Russia in 1980 to study engineering and married a Russian woman with whom he had two children. Unfortunately, like many African students who settled in Russia after graduating, he could not find a job in his field. And he did not want to go back to Madagascar either, knowing the challenges of finding a good job there as well so he stayed in Russia working as a driver for expatriate families.

One day Saïd was driving me to Sidmoi Continent, the local supermarket in our neighbourhood. We would often have interesting conversations in the car about Russia, the people, and the politics. For us, Saïd was more than a driver; he also provided us with valuable, at times unique, insights into Russian culture.

"Saïd, how long does winter usually last here?" I asked.

Tongue in cheek, he smiled, "there are two main seasons in Russia: the green winter in summer and the white winter for the rest of the year."

I shivered, thinking longingly of Indonesia and hibiscus flowers on green lawns.

"During the Russian summer," he said with a laugh, "young women wear skirts so short that they look more like belts!"

According to Saïd, before Gorbachev's *Glasnost* and *Perestroika,* there were Babushkas: big, heavy Russian women. Now, there are Davushkas, the modern fashion-minded Russian woman with stiletto heels and fur coats. For Saïd, this image alone demonstrated the huge upheaval in Russian society after the end of the Soviet empire which opened the door to unbridled capitalism.

The Soviet Union was a communist state from 1922 to 1991 with a highly centralized economy. From 1985 to 1991, Mikhail Gorbachev tried to preserve the Communist Party while modernizing the economy. In a way he wanted to protect the past while caring for the future, an impossible task. On December 25, 1991, Gorbachev resigned and the following day the Soviet Union also known as USSR was dissolved.

Before its dissolution in 1991, the USSR was the largest federation in the world, comprised of fifteen countries: Russia, Estonia, Latvia, Lithuania, Belarus, Ukraine, Moldova, Georgia, Armenia, Azerbaijan, Kazakhstan, Uzbekistan, Turkmenistan, Kyrgyzstan, and Tajikistan.

It is no secret that Russia's current leader, Vladimir Putin, wants to restore the Russian empire to its former grandeur as his final legacy.

Gorbachev was held in high esteem in the western world but was despised in Russia for many reasons. Yes, for dismantling the empire yes but most importantly for attempting to regulate the sale of vodka.

He was succeeded by Boris Yeltsin who opened the door of the Russian economy to oligarchs, this small group of opportunists who became billionaires almost overnight by buying stakes in the natural resources of the country, mostly oil and gas.

So for Saïd, one of the quick signs of Russia's changing society was the difference between the babushkas and the davushkas!

Oly, a Master's student in journalism and communications joined our babysitting team as well.. Oly was bright and really hardworking, she could not sit still for more than five minutes. Later on, like a number of her fellow students, she had a nervous breakdown and had to return to Madagascar without finishing her studies. Her living conditions were just too tough. The Russian government scholarships included free tuition, dormitory accommodation if available and a so-called maintenance allowance that was barely enough for meals. The scholarship did not cover travel costs and other living expenses. Before she left, Oly introduced me to Olivia, another Malagasy student who was living in Voronezh, a small city 100 km away from Moscow.

Like many students, Olivia's meagre scholarship was barely covering her basic needs. She had polio as a child, consequently walked with a pronounced limp. I wanted to help her financially, by providing her with a part time job plus, I felt better knowing we had a backup babysitter for Nicholas. It was the perfect win - win combination!

Olivia had no previous babysitting experience but I was optimistic that she would be motivated to learn. So, we arranged for two afternoon training sessions with Nicholas and the third training session was more or less on her own, on the job. I thought she was ready. Chris and I could finally attend some of the diplomatic events we were invited to but could not accept until now for lack of childcare.

Now that we were organized with childcare, we finally got to enjoy some of the many events happening in Moscow. Moscow wanted to be considered one of the big capitals of the world so the city went out of its way to offer concerts with local or foreign artists throughout the year. One of Chris' favourite bands was the Buena Vista Social Club, an ensemble of Cuban musicians established in 1996 to revive the music of pre-revolutionary Cuba. So, we were delighted to hear that they were giving a concert at one of Moscow's prestigious theatres. We got the medium range tickets at $100 each, and when we got in, we were surprised that the theatre was only half full. We sat in our seats about ten feet away from the stage. Soon after the music started, the usher came to us and gestured for us to move forward, we moved three rows. She gestured further "forward, forward" until we were seated on the very front row, the $600 ones! Apparently, the musicians said it brings bad luck to have the front rows empty, so what a treat for us!

I also went to see Cher with a friend and was dazzled by all the special effects on the stage and Cher herself!

I enjoyed famous Russian ballets like *Giselle* and *The Nutcracker* at the Bolshoi Theatre. After a lonely start, life was definitely starting to look up.

One Friday evening, we went to a dinner party hosted by Kasidis, the head of the United Nations High Commissioner for Refugees (UNHCR) in Russia and his wife Lalita. It was exciting to finally have a social night out with these good friends with whom we had also worked with in China. Lalita was a wonderful cook, and she had a gourmet Thai dinner planned. When we came back, it was past 11 pm and Olivia was still trying to feed Nicholas! Typically, he was in bed by 9:30.

"He does not want to eat," she said casually, facing Nicholas, spoon in her hand.

I felt a little annoyed because I had been hoping that Nicholas would be in bed sleeping by the time we came home. I took my coat off, hung my purse and sat next to her.

"Ok, you can go to bed, I will take care of him."

She said she would rather go to her friend's place because she needed to leave early the next morning. I paid her and she left. I sat opposite Nicholas and tried to force his mouth open just a little. Sometimes he could have a piece of food stuck in his mouth that he did not want to swallow and as a result he would not open his mouth. I gently coaxed my son.

"Nah Nicholas, be nice, open your mouth sweetie."

I carefully slid my middle finger along his lower gum. I felt something rather strange like a tiny piece of wood. I slid my finger over his gum line again. Nicholas moved his head away, obviously in pain. My heart missed a beat, what happened while we were away?

I called Chris to help open Nick's mouth while I looked inside with a flashlight. There was a tiny stick of wood planted in his gum and his front tooth was wobbly. I thought I was going to faint. Chris removed the piece of wood with tweezers, I gave Nick some Tylenol and a bottle of milk. Even though he was a teenager, in times of distress a baby bottle would always soothe him. After I tucked Nicholas in bed, I went to the bathroom and searched around for signs of a fall. I suspected that he must have fallen somewhere. In the bathroom, I knelt down and noticed a small chip on the cupboard under the sink.

With trembling hands, I called Olivia. It was past midnight but I didn't care about the time, I had to find out what happened. I was sad and furious at the same time. Sadness is truly anger infused with hopelessness.

"Olivia, I know Nicholas fell in the bathroom. Would you please tell me what happened?"

I was shouting and shaking at the same time.

She answered meekly, "He was standing in the bathroom. I just left him for a moment to get a diaper from the other bathroom."

I could just visualize the scene: Nicholas standing at the sink with his pants halfway down, waiting to be changed. He must have started to move around, lost his balance, fell and knocked his mouth on the cupboard. I felt so sad for him, for his helplessness.

I hung up, still shaking.

The following day I started to search for a reputable dental clinic. Nicholas had already lost that front tooth in Cairo a few years before when he bumped his mouth on a car door. Kamel, our Egyptian driver acted quickly, wrapped the tooth in a tissue and drove Nicholas to the closest dentist. Amazingly the Egyptian dentist managed to get the tooth back in! The tooth next to it was broken in two and could not be salvaged. At that time, Chris and I were away on a Nile cruise with friends from World Food Programme. Our staff did not tell us anything until we came back because they did not want us to shorten our trip.

I sighed as I recalled the incident. *Poor Nicholas, you poor thing, if only you could express yourself better, you would have called Olivia and said, "Helloo Olivia! Hurry! I am going to fallll!"*

I was mad at Olivia for being careless, but I was also mad at myself. Maybe Olivia needed more training. I should have given her more supervised time with Nicholas. But I was in too much of a hurry to socialize. How could I be so irresponsible?

Tatiana, Chris' assistant, called to say that the Adventist Dental Center had a good reputation among expats and wealthy Russians alike. The dentist was American. He shook his head when he heard how Nicholas had fallen and broken his teeth. After examination, he decided to do a root canal. Nicholas has always had a high tolerance to pain, and the dentist was quite impressed at how smoothly it went. I was relieved!

After we resolved the issue with Nick's tooth, I revisited the idea of adopting a child, possibly a Russian-African child, possibly a girl since we already had two boys. I reflected on a conversation Mike and I had in Cairo when he turned 11 and Christmas was approaching. Out of the blue he asked for a special present: a baby brother. When I told him there was a chance, even a teeny tiny one, that the baby could be like Nicholas, he dropped the subject. I still felt sad for him that he did not get the brother he wished for. I asked Chris what he thought of the idea of adopting a Russian-African child. He was not keen. Too much responsibility, too much uncertainty with our nomadic life. I sighed. This was so disappointing. I just wanted to fix a broken situation.

I knew our family would benefit from a third child. Michael and Nicholas had such different needs they hardly interacted with each other. For me it was like raising two only kids, one a rebellious teenager, the other with multiple disabilities. So Mike did not get his sibling and I did not get my adopted child. I felt irritated and frustrated with my life as a wife and a mother.

In many ways we were a dysfunctional family living in a very dysfunctional country.

One day, while perusing the Moscow Times, I was drawn to a notice about a basket of three puppies, two males and a female, in need of a good home. This was the response of the Universe to my problem! I mentioned it to Mike and he was so excited about the idea.

"Yes, Mom, please please, let's have a puppy"

"Ok, Mike, but we'll have to hide it from Dad as he may say no"

"He'll agree once he sees it, so cute and everything!"

I was so happy to see Mike so excited about getting a furry sibling.

Said drove us to the place where the puppies were being kept. It was at an old university. The lady who welcomed us explained that the puppies were left at their doorstep in a cardboard box. Mike could hardly wait to see the three baby bundles of fur. He picked one up, then another then the third one, undecided.

"Mom, they are all so cute…which one can we have?"

"Mike, actually I think we should take the girl because there are already three males in the house, I need another female presence…"

Reluctantly he agreed, still overjoyed by the new addition.

Mike held the puppy on his lap through the whole trip home, and when she peed on him, it did not dampen his enthusiasm one single bit.

We sneaked the puppy into the house, waiting for Chris 'reaction.

When Chris arrived from work, he did not see the puppy at first but noticed our trepidation, especially Michael's. Finally, Mike could not stand the wait any longer and brought the puppy in.

"Dad, please please can we keep her?"

"OK, I guess this is a fait accompli, we can keep her, but you will have to take care of her entirely…"

"Thanks Dad! Am so happy!"

I decided to call her Shona, an African name, in remembrance of the Russian African child I did not get to adopt.

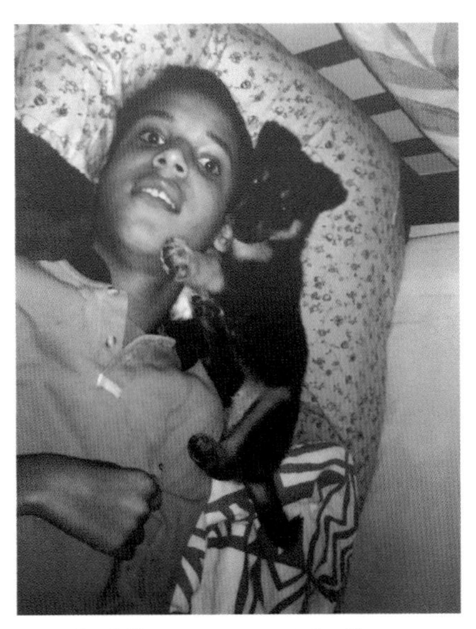

Cuddly moment with Shona

Nicholas before he lost his front tooth

Feeding the pigeons with Masha

THE BIG RUSSIAN MACHINE

Our family continued to settle down in the strange and challenging country that was Russia in 2003-2005.

Through Moscow Accueil, an organization which helps French-speaking expatriates, I found the foreign-run European Medical Clinic and their French-speaking gynecologist, YES! I had to mention some rather intimate issues regarding my decreased libido, so I was glad to be able to confide in my native language. He was welcoming and rather chatty, and after some initial investigation assured and reassured me that as far as he could see, I should not be having any problem in that domain.

"Your tests came back all fine," he smiled. "You should normally be enjoying a fulfilling sexual life."

I sighed: "Well, I am not. Intercourse hurts so it's not very fulfilling, doctor..."

"Thinking about it," he reflected while playing with his pen on his desk," it still amazes me that men and women are sexually attracted to each other because, from a sexual point of view, they are SO very different".

"Let me give you an example," he went on, "a man walking in the street will be attracted by a round behind swaying in front of him, while most women I know will not react at all about how a man walks in front of them. What the women would fall for, would be a caring gesture, or a stimulating conversation."

I laughed. This guy definitely knew women because I, for sure, never paid any attention to how a man walked in front of me and I would certainly run away in disgust if he was swaying his round behind.

"To illustrate my theory even better", he added," in my experience, what counts for men at first sight usually resides below the shoulders and for women, it resides above the shoulders..."

I raised my eyebrows: "You mean, for men, it is the bum and for women, it is the brain?" We both laughed hysterically.

He shrugged his shoulders: "Well, you got it! What can I say? Women are superior, you know, much smarter than we are..."

He sent me home with a prescription for a vaginal lubricant. I still felt skeptical about its benefits, maybe he should talk to Chris about the bum and brain theory.

Because I had been rather pleased with my gynecologist, I went back to the same clinic to see a neurologist for Nicholas, who had started having seizures. This was very disappointing because he had not had any seizures in the last few years. He had stopped taking Vigabatrin, the medication that really helped control his seizures. Nicholas had been part of a pilot group to test the experimental drug in the neuro-pediatric department of the St Vincent de Paul Hospital in Paris. Unfortunately, they found out that one of the side effects of Vigabatrin was vision issues and they stopped it. So now we had to try something else, and I was not sure what. We had been very lucky that Nicholas' seizures had been under control but now that they came back, I was worried as I knew that it often takes a cocktail of two or three different medications to get positive results. Also, it takes time to reach the optimal doses of every medication.

We met with the neurologist, also French, I gave him a bit of the history and he prescribed Gabapentin. I was a bit surprised that he did not schedule an EEG at all. Months later, I learned that he was dismissed by the clinic and expelled from Russia because he was a fake neurologist with false credentials! I quickly checked Gabapentin and to my great alarm found that it is not usually prescribed for seizures but rather for chronic pain! I did not quite know what to do but Nicholas seemed to be doing okay so I left it at that for the time being and made a note to get in touch with his neurologist in Vancouver at the next opportunity.

When I told Chris the story that evening at dinner time, he mentioned Alexei, one of the office drivers. Alexei had been quite sick with pancreatitis and got operated on but did not get better. He kept having infections that were treated with strong antibiotics. He would get slightly better then get fever again. Finally, his doctor ordered an X-ray, and to his great dismay, saw that the surgeon had forgotten a pair of scissors inside. Poor Alexei got operated on again and it took another three months until he fully recovered! We all thought he was not going to make it. Alexei felt like a new man, left his wife to marry a French woman and now lives in the South of France, determined to enjoy his new lease on life.

One time when Nicholas contracted a high fever, I decided to try the local medical system because I was so dismayed with the fake neurologist. I asked Masha to arrange a visit from the neighbourhood doctor. The doctor, a rather grubby-looking man in his 40's arrived at the house at 9 am reeking of vodka. He got into a lively conversation with Masha and recommended that we apply raw slices of onions to Nicholas' back and under his soles. Masha smiled approvingly and went to slice one onion, but I also gave Tylenol for good measure.

When Shona, our beloved puppy who joined our family earlier in the year, got her first period, we all panicked.

Chris was the first to exclaim, "Oh my God, what are we going to do? We can't have her bleeding all over the house. We need to spay her!!!"

Nadia, one of Chris's colleagues who had a dog, recommended her vet. I booked an appointment, but he did not want us to come to the clinic.

"I prefer to come to the house" he said over the phone.

He examined Shona and agreed to come the next day with his assistant to perform the surgery. I was feeling a little uncomfortable, but he said everything would be all right. I just had to prepare some clean bedsheets and hot water and he would take care of the rest.

When he came the next day with his assistant, it occurred to me that we did not discuss where the surgery would take place. He looked around the house and chose Michael's desk.

"This would be perfect!" he said with a satisfied smile.

We cleared the desk of Michael's books to put the bed sheets on it. I brought a bucket of hot water and he told me to leave the room, that he would call me when everything was over.

Two hours later, he came out and handed me a long list for Shona's after-surgery care: antibiotics, vaginal wash, antiseptic, syringes, cotton gauze…

He called me into the operating room, Shona was deeply asleep from the anaesthetic. He grabbed her skin between the shoulders.

"Here, you hold her skin like this and you inject the antibiotics, very easy."

I stared at him, looking blankly. "I have to do this?"

"Don't worry," he said, "very easy…"

As he was leaving, I wanted to write a check, but, no, he preferred cash.

Saïd, the family driver, went to the pharmacy to get the medications. The next day I looked at the instructions, with Saïd translating. So, first apply the antiseptic, then the vaginal wash three times a day, then the injections twice daily and there were a few other things for me to do. I was administering an injection for the first time in my life, my hands were shaking a little bit, and I felt overwhelmed. Her post surgery treatment was to last ten days according to the prescription.

I called my friend Anna for help. She suggested I call the veterinarian at the French Embassy. Bruno, the veterinarian, had been living in Russia for ten years and knew the Russian system quite well. He looked at the prescription and shook his head

"Ha! Typical Russian. They want to kill a mosquito with an atomic bomb!" he said.

He cut the prescription list in half for a week instead of ten days. I breathed a sigh of relief.

Shona standing guard

Apart from issues with doctors and veterinarians, day by day we learned more about how the system works or does not work in Russia as well as our place in it.

I started giving bilingual jewellery-making classes for the expat community and made some good friends among my students. I also joined the African Women in Moscow group and played an active role in their annual bazaar which was held at one of the African embassies.

I was always amazed at the contradiction between the beautiful, extravagant dresses of the African embassy women, and their luxury cars knowing some of them came from some of the poorest countries in the world. Keeping appearances was very important. I actually developed my own theory that the poorer the country, the more extravagant the dresses. The African ambassadors were also members of a solidarity group whose main objective was to put money together in order to assist the unfortunate ambassador who could not return home because of a coup and stopped getting his salary altogether, thus becoming an interesting type of refugee.

Through African Women in Moscow, I met Gladys, from Ghana whose husband was the Cultural Counselor of the German Embassy. Gladys was tall, slim, and beautiful. She was also educated at McGill University in Canada where her dad had been the Ghanaian Ambassador. We hit it off right away, I think what bonded us naturally was also the fact that we were both married to "white" guys! Her husband went on to become the German Ambassador to India.

The African Women of Moscow Group

Joining our social circle were Andre and Agnes Rasolo from the Embassy of Madagascar in Moscow. Andre was the First Counselor at the Embassy. His wife Agnes, as it turns out, oversaw my Catholic Confirmation Retreat when I was in high school in Antananarivo, Madagascar. We were so thrilled to reconnect again after 30 years!

I also became involved in fundraising activities to protect the beautiful Amur tiger of Siberia, on the verge of extinction, with only about 500 left. The movie *Dersu Uzala* depicted the Russian Far East wilderness and heightened awareness about the plight of the Amur Tiger and along with it the vanishing lifestyle of trappers and their environment.

With time, our interest in Russian culture grew and we were fortunate to spend a weekend in Suzdal, one of the oldest Russian towns located on the outskirts of Moscow. I saw this ad in the Moscow Times about spending weekends at an authentic Dacha, like a Russian country house or cottage. Suzdal was founded in 1024 and is the smallest of the Russian Golden Ring towns with about 10,000 inhabitants.

We left Michael and Nicholas with Olianova and we took Said to drive us. The Dacha was rustic but comfortable; it belonged to an American married to a Russian woman. We slept on a big bed heated by a traditional pot of charcoal underneath. In the evening we went to a restaurant where we were treated to tea poured from a samovar, a highly decorated tea urn, traditionally used to heat and boil water. At the end of the evening, a Russian choir, dressed in red and white, entertained us with their beautiful traditional songs. It was a truly mesmerizing experience. Suzdal has many historically important monuments and architectural sites with several of them listed as UNESCO World Heritage sites.

Our trip took place in February and it was bitingly cold, yet this trip stayed in our memory as one of the best experiences of our time in Russia. It gave us a glimpse of the true Russia away from the oligarchs and the Novy Ruski (Nouveau riche). Spending a weekend in the countryside was such a refreshing experience for us. People in the street seemed more genuine and eager to strike up a conversation. I bought a hand-knitted toque and scarf from an elderly lady in thick boots and a heavy coat, a true babushka. She talked to me as if I understood Russian perfectly, and I felt flattered.

On Sunday morning we visited the local church, which Saïd told us Putin would also attend from time to time. It was interesting to watch the devotion of the Russian country folk even after half a century of communism.

On the UN front, Chris was facing his own struggles with the Russian bureaucracy. The World Food Programme had sent 2,800 tons of American iron-fortified wheat destined for Chechnya. Upon inspection of the shipment, the Russian health authorities declared that the wheat was not iron-fortified but iron-polluted, in other words that the iron content of the shipment was too high and poisonous so they could not allow the shipment to be unloaded. In addition, the port authorities in St Petersburg requested one million American dollars for storage fees. Chris negotiated the fees down to $500,000, still a lot of money. In the meantime, he sent samples to an independent lab in England which determined that the wheat was perfectly suitable for human consumption.

"Nyet", said the Russians.

Chris was losing his mind, his patience, his sleep and his hair over the wheat issue. It dragged on for close to a year. Evidently, the real reason was political: The Russians were not going to allow food aid donated by their Cold War enemy to go to Chechnya, a country they have been fighting a brutal war with for over ten years. Chris called his headquarters in Rome for advice.

"What do I do with this wheat? It has been sitting in the port for months with no end in sight and we have to pay daily fees..."

After a week, the response came from his headquarters.

"Send it to Afghanistan! They need it there, plus they have been fighting the Russians..."

Chris breathed a sigh of relief and after another few weeks of negotiation, this time between the Afghanistan office and HQ, the 2,800 tons of iron-fortified American wheat finally left St. Petersburg after eight months stuck in port.

At another time, he got yelled at by an FSB officer. FSB is the government entity that replaced the KGB. FSB raided a Chechen rebel base and discovered bags of WFP food tucked away in a corner. Although Chris' office took great care in delivering food to the rightful beneficiaries, some of it would invariably end up in the hands of the rebels. It was just impossible to control it entirely. The officer called Chris and gave him hell in broken English. Chris played the ignorant foreigner, "Sorry, I don't quite understand what you are saying, can you repeat please..." until the officer, exasperated, hung up on him.

And amidst the glamorous and not-so glamorous events of our Moscow life, there would always be some small event that reminded us of the real reason we were in Russia.

Chris came back from one of his trips to Ingushetia one evening, visibly shaken. He was visiting a refugee camp to assess their needs and noticed this woman pushing a teenage girl in a wheelchair. He asked his assistant about her and was told the mother was widowed, the husband having been killed by the Russian army. Although this was outside the scope of his mission, Chris wanted to visit the mother. They were living in a hut with bullet holes in the walls and mattresses on the floor. The whole situation breathed desperation. With our son Nicholas, we knew how challenging life can be but at least Chris had a good job, and comprehensive medical coverage for himself and his family. Nicholas had access to school and to medical services. In comparison, it was hard to imagine how this widow could manage to care for her special needs daughter in a war zone. Fighting tears, Chris made sure the mother got whatever she was entitled to and discreetly gave her all his cash wondering what else he could do to help.

AIRPORTS

During our two-year stay in Russia, we spent quite a bit of time at airports, flying to Vancouver once or twice a year for the summer and Christmas holidays. Things always happened at airports, always challenging especially whenever we travelled with Nicholas. For example, taking him to the bathroom always required creativity because airplane washrooms were not made for two people and we had to be two people. So the crew would hold a blanket in front of the door because we could not close the door!

Then there was the time when Chris and I were on a flight from Moscow to Copenhagen. We were seated behind a young Russian man who had brought his own bottle of vodka and was drinking from it every five minutes. Finally, the flight attendant told him it was against the rules and he should stop and put the bottle away. He just kept drinking as if he did not hear a word. After a while she came back and told him sternly that if he did not put the bottle away, she would have to tell the captain and confiscate it.

He just kept drinking.

The flight attendant came back, this time with the captain, who told him that unless he gave up his bottle immediately, he would notify the police. The young Russian just stared at the window and kept drinking. As we were landing, we heard sirens approaching the plane. We watched as uniformed men rushed toward the plane and swiftly hauled him from his seat. He was still clutching his bottle.

"See what happens when you don't control your drinking!" I said to my husband.

****

Then there was the time when Mike, Nicholas and I flew from Moscow to Frankfurt on our way to Vancouver. We were to board a Lufthansa flight in Frankfurt and had booked special assistance for Nicholas, so they allowed us to board first. When we were about to sit in our assigned seats, one of the crew members asked us to sit in another place, closer to the washrooms.

"It will be easier for Nicholas," the crew member said with a smile. "We will seat whoever is supposed to sit here somewhere else. I am sure they will understand."

We sat where we were asked to sit. The plane was slowly filling up. A couple walked toward us and looked up at the seat number.

"*Ja, ja*" the man muttered with a heavy German accent.

"*12C and 12D, deese are* ***our seats.***"

"I know," I said while looking around for a crew member, "we were asked to sit here."

"DEESE ARE OUR SEATS," the man bellowed, gesturing for us to get up. ***"Davai, davai, auf auf!***"

He was shouting now, and people were beginning to stare. Mike pulled my hand.
"Let's move, mom."

Finally, a flight attendant came over and tried to explain in German why we were seated in their seats.

"We will give you other seats, better ones, over there..."

"Nein, Nein, auf auf!' The German man wanted none of it, *deese* were his seats, and he wanted them and nothing else.

The crew member became impatient and moved us to some other seats while muttering under his breath, "East Germans, so rude!"

I said it was ok, we did not mind. Later on, after the plane took off, the same crew member came over and said with a wry smile, "Don't worry, it's a long flight - they will suffer!"

****

British Airways and Lufthansa were usually quite good, with special waiting areas for people needing assistance. In Heathrow, the waiting area was aptly called "Serenity Lounge!" Their crew members were also generally very helpful.

Amongst all the airports we came to know, Sheremetyevo Airport in Moscow was the absolute worst. In early January 2004, Nick and I were returning to Moscow from our Christmas holiday in Vancouver. Usually, Chris would leave earlier to return to work and leave me and the boys to enjoy a longer holiday. This time Michael decided to travel with his dad leaving Nicholas and me to travel home together. I was getting used to the long flights, even though looking after a young adult with severe disabilities was always a challenge. We had to be extra organized and book for special assistance and a wheelchair.

An airport attendant pushing a wheelchair was waiting for us at the Sheremetyevo airport. Nicholas sat in it and off we went to go through customs and passport check. The security booths were one floor down so the wheelchair attendant led us to the nearest elevator. His English was basic, as was my Russian. He closed the elevator door and pressed the button to go down. Nothing happened. He pressed again.

Nothing.

"Let's open the door and try again," I said.

The door did not open. We tried various buttons for fifteen minutes, down button, open button, alarm button.

Nothing.

I banged on the glass door to attract someone's attetion.

Nothing.

People were briskly walking by, glancing at their watches. After half an hour inside the elevator, it was starting to feel quite warm. I took off Nick's coat and mine. We pushed the down button again, the open-door button again.

Nothing

I banged at the door; this time really loudly because I had spotted a lady in uniform coming toward the elevator. She stopped at the door.

"We are stuck; can you help us?" I shouted.

She pressed the open-door button, but nothing happened.

"Ok, I am going to get some help," she said.

I felt deep relief and started to put Nick's coat back on. We waited another fifteen minutes. The lady did not come back. I took Nick's coat off again, feeling hopeless. The confined place reeked of vodka; our attendant had obviously been drinking before his shift. I was sweating and started to feel sick. The woman may have forgotten us, or she might have told someone who never bothered to come.

I asked the attendant to bang on the door again, as loudly as he could. Eventually, another woman in uniform came by.

"Please, open the door for us, we are stuck!" I shouted.

She looked at us and shrugged her shoulders. "Sorry, this is not my department."

I was mystified. "So, whose department is it, please?"

"I don't know. Sorry, I can't help you," and she was gone.

Vive le Communisme!

I could have hit her. I felt so tired: tired of the ten-hour flight, tired of this bloody mess of a country, tired of this smelly gentleman and tired of being solely responsible for Nicholas' wellbeing.

We banged at the door again, this time together. A gentleman stopped.

"Are you in trouble? Can I help?" He sounded American.

I asked him to phone my husband and let him know that we were stuck and to please get some help for us. He also tried to open the door but could not. He promised to do his best. I felt like lying on the floor. I wanted to cry. We had just had a ten hour long flight and have now been over two hours at the airport, stuck in this elevator. Nicholas did not have dinner and I was about to lose it and scream. This was too much for my nerves.

I stood in a corner of the elevator not knowing what to do next. I saw our attendant gesturing to a woman. She stopped at the elevator, he said something in Russian. She shook the door lightly, pressed the button and the door opened! She came inside and pressed the down button and down we went! Pfuitt! I could not believe it!

I took Nicholas through the security check in a stupor, collected our luggage and arrived home about one hour later. Chris was watching television. I felt like hitting him. Nick had to be fed and put to bed. After he was tucked in bed, I lay in my own bed repeating to myself, *I can't do this for much longer, can't do this for much longer... can't do this for much longer...*

Defeated, I thought how different my life would have been among hibiscus in Indonesia.

****

In the summer of 2005, Mike was getting ready for his high school graduation. His prom night was special: Together with three other friends, he rented a deluxe limousine. They did not want to be outdone by the kids of the Russian billionaire oligarchs. Something strange happened the day following his prom night. Saïd came in the morning as usual to collect the car keys and warm up the car. He came back fifteen minutes later, a perplexed look on his usually jovial face.

"I don't understand, the car is not parked at its usual place, plus it has no gas in the tank, am pretty sure the tank was full yesterday."

After some investigation, it appeared that Mike had taken the family car for a spin around the city without a driving license and by pure chance managed to bring it back without a scratch, just a few feet away from where it was originally parked!

He graduated in May 2005, with his International Baccalaureate in his pocket, applied and was accepted into the University of British Columbia, Vancouver.

Mike was ready for the next stage of his life. He was getting weary of Moscow's overt racism. While on a school trip to St. Petersburg, he went to a night club with his class and was refused entry in the name of "face control". This is a process where the security guy at the entrance of any establishment could refuse entry to anyone just by the person's appearance! The class stood in solidarity with Mike and they all left to go to a different place.

With Mike finishing high school, this meant I had to take some difficult decisions. After some deliberation, I told Chris it would be best if I moved back to Vancouver with the kids. I could not see how I was going to manage between a rebellious 18-year-old in first year university, a 17-year-old who was nonverbal, could not walk or eat on his own and a husband based in Russia. It was simply too many challenges for me to handle. I knew deep inside my heart that I could not continue to live the life I had been leading for the past 20 years.

For the first time in our nomadic life, I had decided where I wanted to go. In the past, I had always been good at making the best of following Chris and his career posts and creating a life for us in each location. I enjoyed making us a home in each country and even moving furniture around. Each house was very different so turning a house into a home called on my creativity and my inner interior designer. But this time, I was not following Chris. I chose to stay in Vancouver with our kids. It felt so new and strange because I had never done that before.

I longed for Vancouver, to live in the apartment we bought two years before. We only stayed there six weeks every year. I needed to put down roots. I no longer had the physical and emotional strength to meet the constant stress and challenges of moving from country to country, especially with a disabled child.

We left as a family of four in July of 2005 knowing that Chris would return to Moscow on his own. It was the end of an era.

We had been travelling around the world for two decades:

Two years in Mali, West Africa;
Two years in Djibouti, East Africa;

Five years in Rome, Italy;
Four years in Beijing, China;
Five years in Cairo, Egypt;
Two years in Moscow, Russia;

Now the two boys and I would be finally settling down in Vancouver, Canada, the place where I had landed 21 years before. It was the end of a long period of my life. I had travelled extensively, had sat next to ambassadors and heads of state, and met people from all over the world. Now I was preparing to leave this life behind me and embark on a new adventure in Canada.

Chris went back to Moscow in August. He was not quite alone as our family dog Shona was waiting eagerly for him to return. I had also arranged for Sonia, an immigrant woman from Tajikistan, to come twice a week for housecleaning.

I organized our new life in Canada as permanent residents rather than vacationers. Chris and I settled into a type of long-distance relationship, making it work by travelling back and forth between Moscow and Vancouver a few times in that year.

This still required much time and effort, but I felt relieved that at last we were going to stay somewhere for good and I also felt fortunate that we chose Canada as our country of residence. One good thing about our Russian stay was that it made settling down in Canada seem like a breeze, so organized, so logical. Yes, I had to organize Nicholas' schooling and care but for the first time in our lives, we were dealing with professionals:

social workers, teachers, and doctors, whereas in all those other countries I kind of had to be everything: manager, activity coordinator and trainer.

In the summer of 2006, Chris was sent to Darfur, Sudan. I travelled to Moscow one last time to organize the shipment of our personal effects and to close the house. I sold some items, donated others and discarded much. We hesitated about bringing Shona to Canada and I began to look for a new home for her. We placed an ad in the Moscow Times and a newly arrived American family was willing to take her. They came to our house a few times to meet Shona, then we left her at their place for a weekend. They returned her the following day saying she was just too miserable and missed being with us, so we decided to bring her with us to Canada.

Sonia, the cleaning lady, asked me what I was planning to do with Shona.

"I think we are going to take her with us," I said.

"Isn't it complicated, though?" she asked, "With papers and a plane ticket?"

"Not that complicated." I replied, "She just needs some vaccinations, and her plane ticket costs $300.00 - much cheaper than ours."

She fell silent, her head leaning on the vacuum cleaner.

"Sonia?"

She let out a long heavy sigh. As she lifted her head up, she said, "I SO wish I was a dog!"

After Shona arrived in Vancouver and was cleared through customs, her first action on Canadian soil was to relieve herself thus marking her new territory. Then she ran on the green Canadian grass outside the Vancouver International Airport.

I still remember Sonia from time to time, the Tajik woman who so wished she was a dog in order to come to Canada.

Vancouver, Canada, August 2022

ACKNOWLEDGEMENTS

My thanks and appreciation to my friend Shelley Nessman from "The Company of Others" for performing the role of writing coach for the early version of this book.

Thanks to Saïd, Masha, Anya, Tatyana, Oly, Lalao and many others who helped made our stay in Russia not only bearable but interesting as well.

Thanks to my readers: Helena Kaufman, Jackie Weiler, Marguerite Garling, Barbara McLeod and Steve Robertson. Your comments and insights are much appreciated.

Thanks to Helena Kaufman who brought her editing skills to the final version of the book with passion, patience and expertise.

My special thanks to my dear mother-in-law, Marianne Czerwinski, who kept copies of all our letters for 20 years and gave them back to me two years ago. Those letters formed the basis of our family memoir.

Thanks to Chris for providing us with an interesting life even though it was often challenging.

Thanks to Michael who had to deal with the complexities of a nomadic life with a non-verbal brother and a busy mother. Mike, I am sorry for not giving you the time and attention you needed and deserved, will try to make it up for you. Hopefully you will let me.

And of course, thanks to Nicholas, the greatest teacher of all, who brought the best out of me and still does. Life with Nicholas is the life that has chosen me not the one I would have chosen but this life made me who I am today, probably the best possible version of myself.

I also realized that Nicholas did not choose his life either, did not choose to be born with severe disabilities and this breaks my heart. Yet, Nick, you were the most gracious of teachers. You were always in a good mood despite not being able to do things that 90% of the world take for granted: to run, to climb a tree, to enjoy a beer with your buddies, to take your girlfriend to a dance…

When Dr. Olivier Dulac, a renowned French neurologist, told me upon your diagnosis that you were going to be very disabled, I cried for two hours holding your tiny hand. You were four months old then. I wiped my tears and defiantly vowed that I was not going to carry your disabilities as a cross. I will try my best to be happy for you and to keep singing and dancing with you. You taught me resilience and resourcefulness. You gave me some of my best friends. You gave me way more than I could ever give you.

Nicholas was the best ever teenager: no verbal abuse, no drugs except anti-epileptic medications, no alcohol except antiseptic, no junk food except Reese's, his favourite chocolate.

At 34, he still allows me to buy his clothes; he never complains unless he is in intense pain. He loves music, water and car rides making him so easy to please. He pulls your hair and pats your head to show that he likes you. And… he brings the best out of everyone he meets, thus contributing to making this world a more caring one.

So, without you, Nicholas, there would be no story and no book. With your special needs, you turned our expatriate life into a special life, worth telling because I know of no other family who travelled so extensively with a child having such complex healthcare needs.

So, Nick, here's to you, my special child who made me a special parent. Thank you.

Cuddly moment with Momma

Nicholas as a street chic teen of the time